A FRIABLE EARTH

OTHER POETRY BOOKS BY JACKIE WILLS

Powder Tower (Arc, 1995)
Party (Leviathan, 2000)
Fever Tree (Arc, 2003)
Commandments (Arc, 2007)
Woman's Head as Jug (Arc, 2013)

Jackie Wills

A
FRIABLE EARTH

PUBLICATIONS
2019

Published by Arc Publications,
Nanholme Mill, Shaw Wood Road
Todmorden OL14 6DA, UK
www.arcpublications.co.uk

978 1911469 94 0 (pbk)
978 1911469 95 7 (hbk)

Design by Tony Ward
Printed in Great Britain by
Printondemand Ltd

Cover picture:
'Allotment' by Jane Sybilla Fordham
by kind permission of the artist

ACKNOWLEDGEMENTS
Poems have appeared in *The Rialto*, *Magma*, *The Dark Horse*,
The North, *Mslexia*, *Warwick Review*, *The Needlewriters Anthol-
ogy*, *The Level Crossing* (Dedalus Press), *Killer Whale Journal*,
Poetry Salzburg and *The Golden Shovel Anthology*. 'Brother'
won 1st Prize in the 2015 Wenlock Poetry Competition, 'Let-
ter from Vévé' was shortlisted for the 2017 Keats Shelley
Prize. 'Notes on an Expedition to Mexico' won 1st Prize in the
Sentinel Literary Quarterly competition 2016.

Editor for the UK & Ireland
John Wedgewood Clarke

CONTENTS

LAST SMEAR

Is there a quota of love for each of us, I wonder
on the examining bench, my question
something to do with how much rain has been falling
and no-one next to me in bed. That rain has broken records.
A desire not to be alone is widespread in January.
Dating sites swell with singles. All ages and preferences.
When I bump into Sandra on Lewes Road she's adamant.
What does she need a smear for? She's given up sex.
I fill that space with a book. None of this passes
between me and the nurse (although our boots
are almost identical). She finishes, cheerful, *that's it,
no more smears for you*. It's been nearly forty years,
this protracted relationship with the speculum.
Is it already time for last things? Clouds rolling in, creamy,
pigeons taking advantage of the wind to curl and dive,
the phone line swaying to its own out-of-time lyrics.

SPIDERS DROP FROM MY HAIR

I carry them down the hill from the allotment
where, as I bend, they fall from raspberries,

are blown off plum and elder trees on fine lines,
ready to spin webs. When they abseil

from my head my house accommodates
them in the corner of a frame or cavity

below a chest of drawers and there they grow,
extending their traps, waiting. Perhaps, like me,

they miss the places they've left,
unadventurous travellers, unwittingly removed.

WATERING

The young man living in his silver Honda
answers through a rear window he has all
he needs – a blanket, empty box
of fried chicken. I smell tobacco, he looks
back at me through sunglasses, stretches, *yes*,
he says and *no* and *thanks*, I say *take care*,
go to water onions and potatoes,
the earth so dry it blots up my false rain.
A blackbird flaps in the spray. Water runs
down his car windows too, as fog, and proof
he's alive. What can he tell me, looking
in? That each night he breathes out a fraction
more of himself, while a rose straggles up
a stake and bags of compost lie on beds
like pillows – a young man between blossom-
stout trees and barbeques biding their time?
I saw him first, thin as the trench I'd dug
for earlies and want him to know how close
he is to badger paths, that here hedges
warble, the city's staggered roofs house chicks
who mew like cats, how earth sends back the sounds
of rakes and spades, that *you* and *me* can blur
somewhere in between. I want him to know
the old elms are preparing to loosen their seeds
and when they fall the streets feel softer,
that there's an empty shed and fresh water.

LIFE EXPECTANCY

In the two hours one woman's voice filled Carriage F
I wasn't thinking of all the deaths,
I was straining to see through a patch of window
allocated to my seat, which didn't seem enough.
My sightline was blocked and her voice was there

when I dozed and woke, denouncing the student
who drove into her security gate and the landlord she'd sue.
I tried to visualise a gate between two gable ends, the margins
of modern executive homes and private parking,
separated by holly and wood chip, which made up her view.

She described where the CEO sat, described the chair.
Even then I wasn't thinking of the deaths, nor
when she handed her three-month baby over, weaned,
to a sister-in-law, not even as she listed all her team's
achievements. I looked for lambs and rivers,

let the passing green blur into me and felt my body break
down, as if there were two of us – me and it – my body separating
into bits that would fail. All the deaths came blowing in –
the way a pheasant's tail feather is carried from a field,
comes to rest between the tracks at platform eight.

BECOMING AN AGE-DEFYING CREAM

Closer than a lover lying skin
to skin, I'm lanolin on an old ewe, huddled
in a sheepcote against driving snow.

I BUILD A HOUSE OVER MYSELF

A house of scraps, sewn on an old treadle machine,
making bricks stuffed with underwear.
My house will do, one day, as a soft room
where I can throw myself against the walls.

BEING A CRATE

I picture myself at the docks
full of oranges or bananas, home
to a tarantula, stuffed with straw, stamped
with a red, yellow, blue label
from the Tropic of Capricorn.
Emptied. Filled. Empty. Full.

BECOMING MY HAIR

Badger, my friend's husband called over the wall.
First I thought of corpses on the way to mum's,

then their sounds, playing at night in the street,
their paths through summer raspberries,

the sweetcorn they have such a taste for.
I was on all fours, by then,

knocking down rows of broad beans, feasting.
The damage I could do.

VÉVÉ'S INVITATION

He found a small farm outside Cherbourg –
visit he urges but it's too late.

Vévé's invitation has been unanswered
for decades and he doesn't send an address.

Would I find him ready for less,
like I am, his arms full of logs,

content with a Calvados or playing the Gibson
he wants prices for?

I'd tell him how Dan turned up in leathers,
his hands bloody and cut,

every window in the exam hall collapsed
onto cobbles –

itinerant fire-eater, Dan, and Vévé his beacon,
putting up with his drinking, his friends.

My cat paws at a wasp on the window.
Vévé writes to another me brought up on saints,

but I'm forgetting their names.
Is he the man (with his brotherly kisses)

to ask if Dan's eating raw chilli with the dead?
Was he the one to show me the way?

FLOATERS

In the eye hospital my dilated pupils must convince
the old rollerblader opposite I'm there to elope
to the Iguaçu Falls where two countries meet –
my body's last adventure. *Are you single?*
He mentions his lovers and my pupils are floodgates,
my past gushing back in the glare a nurse warned of.
Before we can swap numbers he's called to a doctor,
me to another, who describes the spots, barbed wire,
flashing lights, oscillating at the edges of my sight,
as *floaters* – shadows on the retina, the debris of age.
I put on dark glasses to head home, my eyes plunge pools
for late love that's detained in a consulting room,
as a village leaves its mountaintop to jiggle in the flow
of a great river, a leaf twists from a twig in a gust.

GLAMOUR

When Sylvester Stallone pulled a hair
from a mole on my cheek he had a film look
on his face as if the trophy between his fingernails
was a threat worthy of Rambo. His gesture
was so intimate, his reach so fast, his pincer grasp
so accurate, I could imagine him perfecting that action –
see, pinch and pull in one move – for hours. And I admit
I've been studying how to remove hairs on my upper lip.

But women with dark crescents above their mouths
crowd into the magnifying mirror to accuse me
of betraying them – women who refuse to pluck,
wax, thread, depilate, epilate, shave or save
for laser treatment. They tell me Stallone
appeared in my dream as old Norse fighter, Thor,
defeated at wrestling by Elli, Giant Crone,
and his tweezerhand's a last sullen kick at the door.

AMP

i.m. Linda Rickett

Linda, the amp you sold me when you left still works.
It seems wrong a black box outlives you, however good the make.
I couldn't count the songs it's played since you got rid of everything.
The studio you taught dance in's boarded up, a wreck
you wouldn't want to see. I always struggled with my feet,
even simple patterns, but you reiterated, *one, two, three,*
when my left wouldn't follow. Wednesday nights,
floor to ceiling mirrors played it back exactly as it was.
Just outside, on the Steine, heading for the pub or home or sea,
men and women passing by would have overheard your tracks
and for a moment, moved a little differently. The mirrors
that repeated us are dusty now, shattered into stars. But in my amp
I hear your tracks – and underneath the album in my hand
is your hand directing me, your feet introducing the next routine.

TORTOISE

I have begun to recognise myself in profile
as a tortoise and watching one tortoise
flip another from rolling helmet onto its feet
I wonder if I'm the one who's lost balance,
stranded, waggling my leathery neck,
staring at the sky and rocking
until something arrives to turn me over,
show me the earth again

or if I'm the rescuer, steady follower
of long-distance paths –
if it's my job now, to tip the stranded
back on track, a guide of sorts.
So I plod on, crossing borders with a name
painted on my shell, knowing anything
might topple me as I amble among hazards,
grazing flowers, wild grasses and greens.

Somewhere there's a dump of wasted time,
where starting and not finishing, late trains,
queues at a till are lobbed into shipping containers

with time spent staring at TV dramas, free papers,
doodles and mirrors, to meet the hours waiting
for repairs, on hold, re-negotiating a contract.

How many ways could I waste it? And is that
what the cat does – going out, coming in
and going out again? Or watching nests being built?

Half-hearted to the last, I couldn't name
one important time-waster of the past.
Who wastes time the best, is there a prize

or fellowship? An Order of the Sheepskin Slipper?
I'd like to think the worms will deal with it,
my squandered decades passing through a blind

pink streak, living in the dark, so that wasted time,
in time, like lettuce out of date or bolting,
will turn itself into the real thing, where it began.

HYSTERICS

Like the time neighbours put a hoop on their wall
I feel the ball rise in my throat (*globus hystericus*).

I swallow and my heart thuds. It's with me
for days, this thumb on my neck

that's less a lump than an eye looking back,
replaying near misses, the eye of a woman

in a line, hands on her hips,
who cleans toilet rims, pays children's debts,

whose fears are among friends,
beside motorways, in microwaves.

OLD WOMAN GORGE

Have you heard about the oldest old?
How no-one quite agrees when old starts
anymore,

how often the rarest specimens
are photographed: the oldest footballer,
oldest and fattest president, oldest dog,
oldest poppy seller, the oldest mother,
oldest horse or cat.

It's marvellous, the food they eat,
the years they survive beyond a century
on rice gruel, raw eggs, smoking, drinking
and being single.

    (Old Woman Gorge: distempered cliffs,
    stricken trees hanging on above a stream,
    rocks oxidating in painted caves,
    the oldest city, Damascus, city of lace,
    its gates of peace and paradise.)

And did you know *I, we, ashes, flow*
are the earliest human words,
with *mother, spit* and *old?*

LETTERS FROM CONNECTICUT, 1988

I've lived nowhere but here, never more than two hours
from where I was born, my radius a day return.
Once I met a man who refused to leave his valley, afraid
of who he'd be without the brush of aniseed and wild thyme.

Your letters are from 3,000 miles away, long envelopes
to an address I'd half-forgotten with tall windows
and wooden floors. In them – news of AIDS
and names of bands. You ask if crack's arrived in the UK,

describe how *two ounces of cocaine was found submerged in the oil
of the deep fat fryer* at a local club. You predict a Bush victory
will surpass Thatcher's sins. I read all three again,
needing to suspend today. How did we feel old at 34?

I feel your eyes on the massed Mercedes of Greenwich wives
collecting husbands from the New York train. I hear your smirk
as you describe the boss's last memo: *Call the Donofrio bitch.*
And then I stand with you at the edge of a remote ravine

the spot you returned to *countless times between the age of four and six.*
You recount *the terrible urge to jump* and I see it – a cleft of bushes
interrupted by rocks, a waterfall, some gliding bird, the silver
scratch of river so far down carrying childhood's white stones.

CONSIDERING I'LL BECOME MUD

It's time to pay attention to microbes
colonising the dark matter of humus and loam,
to the impossibility of knowing who was here before.
I've howked soil like Sussex cattle at a gate,
I've beasted it, breaking it up for years,
standing on the spade, raising broken bones,
disrupting the useful work of dandelions – so for the sake
of snegs, ammots, tap roots and Vasily Dokuchaev,
classifier of gubber and gawm, who mapped soils
in river beds and steppes, I'm done with digging.
I'll treat my beds as beds, soft enough to lie in,
for the sake of women, men and all our children.
And in time, my two will mix me with this wormy,
friable earth, conducted by the cutty's goistering.

Note: *gubber* and *gawm* are Sussex dialect words for mud. *Howk* means
to dig, *beasted* means tired out, a *sneg* is a snail, *ammot* an ant, a *cutty* is
a wren and *goistering* is loud feminine laughter. Vasily Dokuchaev was
one of the first soil scientists.

ALLOTMENT

Ian's fire burns below the mist. I watch him snaffle
a length of plank from another plot and hear it crack.
The moon above the road is blurred, I'm cold
and it's too dark to dig. The day hovers over strips of soil
I uncovered forking weeds from between the currants.
The finches have left the tops of trees to a salt wind.
There's not a cat in sight, or human, just Ian in his half-shed.
I wander to his flames. We list the coffee shops on Lewes Road,
calculate the grounds they could provide, discuss nitrogen,
big bud, leather jackets, wireworm. Our tiny farms,
approximations, are so hungry – there's barely a foot of earth.
But garlic's poking through and endive survived the frosts. I cut
at kale, rearrange a veil over purple-sprouting broccoli.

Yes, sometimes it's too much, keeping track
of what grows best with what, why the sage died
why tomatillos failed. From March, I'll work in line
with Jeanette, Bridget, Dave, Matt, Angie and Rob,
sewing our rows, potatoes chitting at home.
Blackberries will throw ropes of thorns, blackbirds fill
their beaks with worms, one spade will dislodge weeks
of work by ants, bees will fly from hives by the mast,
moths hover, grey, slight in the raspberries and in time,
on the path, four wrens will prove the ecstasy of parenting.
Then long days of tea and glut, beans, fear of blight,
squirrels scrumping plums, and once, a hummingbird
hawk moth feeding on bergamot. I'll scout for mirabelles,

the sweetest harvest, on abandoned plots where oregano
reaches high as rosebay willowherb, where travellers settle
each summer and below the canopy, anyone could bend a den
dry enough for sleep. They're what I'll miss, with my strip of land
from road to cemetery, its winter squash, early rhubarb
and the moment one courgette plant becomes a factory,

kneeling by broad beans just for the scent, lavender
buzzing for weeks, heady elderflowers, the drink I make
and save for Christmas. This is my reason, birds
decreeing plants to life, spiders sticking my hands
to leaves, the old bath churning with prehistoric tails,
yellow trumpets, blue borage stars, calendula's healing crowns,
mint bunched and drying, the steadiness of seeds.

TOAD

When the sound, *hag,*
is thrown from the green transit
towards my open window,
emptying its rhymes *fag, bag, nag, slag,*
I envy Toad his stolen cars,
hooting down single-track roads –
his ultimate disguise
an apron and a headscarf.

SLOWWORM

Like girdles, which Anne Lincoln's mum
sold in the Army and Navy, tights now come
with fingers of spandex to keep you firm.
Rolling them on, you feel the biscuit fat even

out, your shilly-shallying belly replaced by scales,
until you emerge, pure body, pure tail,
from under a tree trunk into the night, surprising
yourself – quick, golden and muscular again.

SLEEPING TO OWLS

If I entered this talk between owls,
their short, long, short, long, calls,

I'd be a vixen scaling walls
to scream my young back,

I'd wake as a cow licking my calf
into life. I'd never come back

from the corner of a barn
where old wheels are flung,

my own cedar wood confessional.
I listen in a high, soft bed,

witness the window fill and drain,
hold my breath with the undergrowth.

WANDERING WOMB

The womb is often out of its natural and proper place*

It's the size of a mouse or turtle,
can turn itself inside out like a glove.
No surprise then, it wanders,
if you think of how a glove conducts
a choir and all the places a mouse
or turtle might visit, compared to a womb,
which is now joined in its ambling
by a kidney, eye, spleen, all of them nomads
seeking relief from a 24-hour contract
to remain in the same body.
Tell me, is it cruel to tempt my womb
(of all body parts) back to captivity,
and anchor it with stitches
to this body-zoo, *it's natural and proper place?*

* *Virtues Household Physician,* 1927

NO NEWS

Just walking up the hill
to pick greens

no news in the shed
no news in the family

bumping into a friend or two
no news

some work here and there,
but no, *no news*

one day there's wind
another, sun, a river joins an estuary

to its spring and back again
no news composing itself

before knocking on my door
just walking down for bread

no news in the cat's yowl
or the clock's hands

just opening the curtains
to see what sort of day it is

no news, a gang of sparrows
sings, in the hedge next door

ON NOT MAKING IT TO THE PEAK, SOLOMON

i.m. Solomon Odeleye

Lizards scuttle off the path, undergrowth
crackles with paws or hooves.

The smoke of forest fire lingers in the scrub
as I pass a grove of old, pale trees,

bending over a fallen trunk.
The way to the peak is blocked, Solomon

so I refuse to climb any further, even though
the moon is full and it's your funeral night.

On the track twisting back to the village
I step over shadows as you did, thinking them solid.

How does it compare, the only landscape you saw
before asking *who's pulled the curtain*?

You were four – but now, on the southern tip
of your continent, among leadwood and guavas,

the moon on a grass roof reminds me
of our walk up a mountain in Yorkshire,

five or six of us, behind a farmhouse rented for a week.
It started to snow. You stopped by a rock,

faced the storm's blank view and wouldn't go on.
You could outargue anyone, so we left you alone,

until a party of walkers came out of the blizzard
and showed you the way down. It's winter here too

and a tornado the other night could have been you,
visiting. Are you that white-breasted bird resting on a log?

Or the leafy-winged bat I watched disappear
into the lace of moon, mountain and forest?

VHO MJEDZI

Vho Mjedzi is sinewy as a vine
anchored to the limb of the century
she was born in.

And most of the day she sits
on a log by our zozo
of wood and tin in her Paul Smith t-shirt,

donated by a gap-year boy. Her English
non-existent – and why not –
she bends her knees out of habit, saying *kissimus*,

and cups her hands in
the Venda woman's way,
knowing I'll send one of the children

to the tin for biscuits, balance the kettle
between stones round the fire.
Now she beckons,

loads water drums into a wheelbarrow.
We bump in and out of ruts
cut by storms to stand at the tap. Vho

Mjedzi's showing me off
kindly as we queue, joking about how little
I know – no words in my mouth

for how to lift 20 litres
onto my head, no words for corn, spoon, orphan,
goat, cooking pot, peanut butter,

no words for the sleeping sickness
that comes home from Polokwane
and Gauteng on the bus

with more and more married daughters
and sons, no words for palliative,
cure, for the liquor store

selling single cigarettes, where men drink
until the quartz hillside thunders
with kwaito. Whatever she thinks

of me but can't say, whatever I want
to ask her but don't know how,
is shaped by the log, by biscuits we dunk

into Rooibos, signs we make with our hands,
lines sketched in dust. We manage.
What's lost returns to hang

over the woods each morning, hiding
from both of us the thick-tailed bushbaby
and red forest duiker.

It's untranslatable as a mother's
breath on the fontanelle,
drains into Vho Mjedzi's earth,

and settles in an aquifer, held
pure in the space between rocks, far below
hollows we both dig here for the dead.

JOHANNESBURG 2012

after a line by Gwendolyn Brooks –
'A Black boy near Johannesburg hot in the Hot Time'.

Approaching the turn-off for Gold Reef City, is a
bridge where your grandmother had her pitch. Black
hair wrapped in a Venda woman's pink cloth, you still a boy,
she sold sweetcorn grilled over charcoal. We're so near,
its yellow country smell rewinds four decades. Your Johannesburg
is the routes you ran to Soweto, chased from Rocky Street hot
with cops. Later, as a choir sings on waste ground in
Hillbrow, a mechanic stares and shouts, *stay on the
road*. No-one walks here – we're black, white, mixed. Hot,
dusty, we're exhausted by apartheid. Still. Beating. Time.

AXES

I hear dogs hunting at dawn, the puppy whimpering
outside our door. A boy from the village has taken its mother.
Around the fire last night we listened to the two of them
crash through the bush, the puppy yelping, trapped somewhere.
Was she teaching it her paths, where bush pigs graze?
We shone torches and called, threw bones into the dark.
Now the pup cringes out of reach. I find leftovers, persuade
it to stay with me when everyone leaves – and all afternoon, axes

knock at the bark, the heart of wild fig, ironwood, sweet thorn,
violet trees, that contain cures for everything: wounds, cuts,
eyes closed by pus, gonorrhoea. Cures are not what these men
are here for, disturbing the bush-baby in its hollow, risking hornets
and wild bees. They leave villages where trees have vanished.
Their rhythm keeps perfect time – certain as hunger and thirst.

WITNESS

for Mrisi and Giya

The leopard mother appears at dawn, her cub
behind the long curve of her tail,
her coat of rosettes the only one on earth
and dawn holds them both in the shadows

of the Tropic of Capricorn, admiring them.
Here's the elephant highway, here are kudu horns
spiralling into a spike, and buffalo staring
out of the bush, here are watering holes.

She paralyses her prey with a bite, strangles it
with her jaws, drags her kill into a leadwood,
sinks her muzzle into a springbok's heart,
calls her cub with grunts. She suckles between hunts,

keeps it hidden for weeks, guarded by darkness
and the treaty sunlight makes with trees.
We're looking for lions or rhino in our flimsy car,
expecting baboons, turn into a remote, dusty loop.

She steps out of the scrub the way the old flag, folded
in a drawer, still waves in the old wind. She won't leave.
She's there when we encounter two elderly Afrikaaners
by a baobab at Mopani camp, one leading the other

along a stony path, their trainers unproven,
not yet broken in. She watches with me as they read
the tree's history, discuss what birds roost here,
quick to condemn the old regime, ask what we've seen.

We start with the leopard and her cub by the dry Shingwedzi.
Once in a lifetime, the men agree. My daughter says nothing
about black capital letters on white asbestos –
that would have told her where she couldn't stand or sit.

All we have or haven't witnessed comes to rest
under the baobab – the leopard mother, her grunt,
untold places we'd have never been allowed to enter once,
all four of us.

In the car park of Phiphidi Falls, an office choir's singing
and clapping hands, arranged in a crescent as if in church.
It's their cleaner's leaving do. Like us, they've brought food.
We leave them the shade, they spill beer and pray.

At the Mutshindudi River, gnarled and knotted
trees, tattooed with water, grow hollow to catch
summer's floods. Birds slide notes through wood,
towards a plunge pool below the longest drop,

where last year a woman drowned. Feet caught,
she grabbed for clouds. Waterfall repeats waterfall,
rocks flattened by months of rain, the force of springs
flowing into streams, filling tributaries, claiming the gorge

until no jagged edge survives. Like lovers, a congregation
moved their feet in rhythm baptising her. Like lovers,
they heard the wood dove and the bunting.
When she failed to rise, they found hymns.

We hear their harmonies in leaving songs. We hear her
carried to the road for Sibasa. We hear blessings as verges burn
all the way to another dammed river that will never reach
the sea. More rain will come, the waterfalls promise.

ROAD FROM THE NORTH

for Risenga

to each side of it, birds
and children imitating birds
coal and platinum
half the world's families of spiders
and the endangered Martial Eagle
giant cabbages outgrowing
their ochre beds

the Tropic of Capricorn interrupts it

shadows, fires and suitcases
for Soweto, Makado or Polokwane
donkeys, houses of tin
built on macademia nut husks
to each side tumbling marula fruit
bananas and grapes

a roadblock interrupts it

women carrying nets of oranges
on their heads or baskets of chickens
a woman with reeds for her roof
a woman with branches cut
from a smouldering forest
a woman with a crumpled bag
of maize pounded into flour

a herd of cows interrupts it

on one side, bowls of wild spinach
and ground peanuts
to both sides of it, stalls hung
with tomatoes and small, brown,

creamy avocados
lorries straining under brieze blocks,
cement and sand, coaches, taxis,
over-loaded with pots and blankets

a toll gate and services
Gauteng interrupts it

a barricade interrupts it

heavy snow interrupts it

farmworkers, rubber bullets
and burning vines

AS WE DRIVE AWAY FROM ORANGE FARM

they walk out of the night, following a fence,
an invisible path, or halting at crossroads
to hold cigarettes for sale, one by one, invisible

until they're close enough to touch.
The road and night roll together in dust,
releasing people into cities, onto empty verges,

reveal them in twos, alone – a man
made into a giant by the trolley he pulls,
a woman whose child is a curve on her back.

Thin men in tracksuits are dark as the charred
marshlands they cross. They are you and me,
strangers to everyone, alive only in headlamps
            between here and there.

PLAYING SCRABBLE AT THE DEATH CAFÉ

My old friend has taught the monkey in his lap to pour
a Domaine Leroy Richebourg Grand Cru without spilling
a drop. His Dombey Street neighbour is folding up
a white cane and reciting the rules of Scrabble.

The board's in Braille and the blind man's denying
he's a cheat. They toast Dante re-writing Inferno
at the next table and Blake sketching souls ascending.
An undertaker's manual props open a door to the garden,

with a study into the last rites of a forgotten people
buried with carob seeds. My friends are competing
for a triple word score, calculating, as an hourglass empties,
turns, empties again, the values of RAZE, ZAP, EXIT,
QUELL, QUASH, MARMALIZE or CRUCIFIXION. *Oh man,*
one says at BANJAXED, makes the best of it with DEAD.

SKUNK

after Robert Lowell

She bought sleepers, retired from the weight of trains,
to raise beds for runner beans behind her tall hedge.
They shoot red flares at us in summer, crawling
up their canes. And her son paces the street,
examining leaves so closely for blemishes and veins.
I was climbing the hill tonight after 48 hours of bad coffee

and remembered our street shrouded in skunk,
how the smell appeared like fog rising from the marina,
out of drains, boarded and forgotten wells,
neighbours sniffing the air as if it was spring.
A broken Vent-Axia, a dormer left open –
it was unmistakeable. For two days we woke to it.

Anyone waiting for a bus, kids on their way to school,
breathed it in. It lingered in Bernard Road
and Totland, round the cemetery gates like a mongrel.
The young man who walks like a monk, considering
his next step for as long as it takes to buy bread
and get home *is not right*. But nor am I.

My head's full of politicians,
I can't turn the radio off, it empties endlessly
into the graves. Just before Christmas,
his mother, skinny as an heiress, stopped me
by the offie. Fairy lights drooped in a window
and dangled from a blueish tree

as she described the pavilions of her son's mind,
how she laid down lines of stones for him,

unwound silk thread, strung it between lampposts
to mark his path, keyed their postcode into the GPS.
At the kitchen table, he would stare at her
as if they were on opposite banks

of a wide river growing into an estuary –
an ebbing, flowing stain. I stand at the window at 4 am.
Outside, badgers are playing – cubs chitter
under dark cars, while by the passion flower hedge,
that clings on, displaying its wounds and nails,
the mother keeps watch, keckers and yelps at them.

One department held spitting contests, players chewing paper
to project onto the wall of a neighbouring school. We laid bets
on how quickly a junior would cry in the place anything
might be spiked, Mel, in Victorian underwear, threatening
to set a slacker's pubes on fire. The boss sat in his office,
studying insects, listening to opera on headphones.

When we went on strike the country froze. We grouped at gates
to stop deliveries, drove to pickets to be rescued from baton swings
by stronger members of the NUM. A resident of St Mungo's,
opposite head office, joined us on the snow-packed company steps.
We shouted for better pay and he alerted us to legions of beetles
crawling towards the double doors. The MD called the police on us.

To mark our struggle, I honour these two insect men – one
smooth-shaven, nearly bald, the other wild-haired, bearded
to the third button of his coat, men who knew a glow-worm
converted prey to liquid, wasps chewed wood to make a nest of paper,
men who understood how a Psyche caterpillar wove its cloak,
men, who in studying insects, were considering the soul.

EUROPEAN FIRE ANT

It's one of those rare hot days – rain's forecast tomorrow –
when compost falls away and the rope of yellow nettle roots
isn't so hard to loosen. The afternoon hesitates.
Ants scramble onto my gloves. Purposeful, they're tending
a herd of aphids on the artichokes, milking them for honeydew.
The European fire ant trades protection for food,
is studied for its corpse carriers and paths.

My spade slices through a nest. The soil teems, speckled
with pupae, glinting with ants rushing to the rescue.
I stop digging, here's a labyrinth – alive, organised,
built like a brain. An expert navigator, the fire ant's colonised
the world in container ships, surviving far from anchorage,
in the offing, on the horizon. Which is where I still
mourn you because we had that in common, the sea.

And something else in this shattered nest makes me think
of your lit window in a warren of terraces, and Hecate,
midwife of exits and entrances, Persephone's companion.
Perhaps it's an underworld joke, how some butterflies survive?
Their larvae secrete a disguise, are dragged underground
by the ants, who feed them like cuckoos until they are fit
to crawl out of their chambers and unfold their blue wings.

LETTER FROM MY FATHER

When my father left for Brazil, in the days international calls
were rare as telegrams and there was no email, he posted me
a letter containing his will. It lay on my doormat, large, brown,
official, my address an oblong in fountain pen, each word
leaning forward like an old fence in the wind. I thought
he loved travel, but each new flight lifted him above the flocks
preparing to migrate and what happens to a heart at the limits
of atmosphere? He'd flown so much I think he knew it
was giving notice and might decide, anytime, in a bar or jewellers
in Rio, at a beach hotel, or as he fought the Atlantic undertow,
to take off like a warbler, quietly, unnoticed. He'd be stateless,
somehow, by dying on business. Unequipped to express
any of this he sent his will, to arrive when he was in the air,
heading towards Brazil's amethysts with his unsteady pulse.

ROB'S SHED

He's been sick almost a year and today
his plot is criss-crossed with nasturtiums,
looped between apple trees, peach, pear,
like a net below a tightrope to catch the fallen,
strung with orange, red, yellow – and glowing.
If he could see this scramble of plate-sized leaves,
pale stems still stretching towards a spur
to hold fast, if he could lie among these open-
throated flowers that sing to his paths,
as he used to daydream in his hammock.
I stare into a beech windbreak. With sun behind
and breaking through, it's an ingot. Look, Rob,
at the shine, how the blackbird folds itself
and settles on a vine hanging from your porch.

LONELY

The old travellers' camp is empty,
hard-standing scorched,
scattered with twists of metal
and insulation the colour of medical waste.
Someone's been burning a shed.
By the blazing hips, sloes are ripe.
Starlings and gold crests spray glitter songs,
a walker calls her dog pack
to a fistful of leads.
Who'd carry a shed here –
over concrete security barriers,
down chalk ditches, to set it on fire?
My city's Google searched *lonely*
so often we've become a statistic.
Remains of the shed wait like stretchers
for us and whoever else visits in the night.
It's easier to talk about chlamydia
than to admit, *I'm lonely*. I came for elder,
the valley was stripped. The sloes
are buffed with cloud. My secret.

CANAL CANDIANO

for Jane Fordham

We freewheeled to the canal's empty warehouses,
stopping at the customs gate. Loose fencing clattered
against wild bamboo. A cormorant cruised in, a row
of brown-headed gulls hesitated on the wall. The storm
had brought jellyfish, nearly transparent moon bags
branded with circles like buttonholes, skirts pulsing.

There was one fisherman and us, watching them surface,
somersault, lengthen and contract in the clear water,
they were all sizes, blown from a deeper sea,
where tides oscillate, water bulges with white galaxies,
puffs of static, shot through with silver filings
almost too small to see.
                    The wind scattered more grit
and jellyfish mimed their incomprehensible phrases,
turning in the current like a plane's disappearing vapour trails.
The fisherman shook them out of his net. Mostly water,
stilled, they shone like eyes as we looked through them
to the verge – their bloom, their moon-tints, gone.

HOUSE MARTINS

Stinking of fox, Julie's dog sprints uphill and I follow
until I hear house martins heading for the sea.

The hill empties. They bolt
out of turf, drop towards the sheep.

One pair skims the dog, who's watching me watch
them stream

away from us – a second flock, a third. Stragglers drop
to the tip, vanish over the beach.

The dog waits, I say, *They've gone*.
In the interval only migration or a storm can leave –

charged with plant oils, the taste of soil worn
into a path, with salt and spores – the sky's bereaved.

BROTHER

i.m. Major Michael Wills

You are blurred on a path by the river, Waverley abbey ruins
on the opposite bank, where a wren picks up the speck of a chant

and stone windows arch over turf. We walk, the dog kicking up leaves.
In your camouflage jacket, you blend with trees and moss

as you meander away from Mum and me. You were dead as we
    drove west,
past a vast excavation of chalk feeding the voracious moon,

past Stonehenge. That moon kept the van on the road until we
    arrived.
And from a terrace, waiting for permission to see you,

Mum willed the sun to come up. It sent a column of light over Devon,
over the Cessna broken in a field – a pillar made by ice crystals
    as they fell

from cirrus clouds. We hadn't spoken for years. Not about Dad's funeral,
our camps, the half-decade between us, the eclipse, your sky diving

and Elstead's resident kingfisher. We were invisible to each other,
lying low in our childish woods. But this is a leap year and it's February.

I know you've been back, pumping swings on the rec, splashing
down the stream. Today's yours – it always was – and I wish we could
    traipse

the sandy tracks round Frensham Pond, over Hankley Common,
that the rift fracturing us was a gully we'd jump for a dare.

COMMEMORATIVE STAMP

Concorde's boom was the future crossing. She changed the sky,
took the Vulcan's delta wings, her engines, left silence behind.

Earth ruptured, gardens slid into voids. Wild birds flew up in
    alarm.
In classrooms, kids bent the noses of paper planes. To charm

sound like that, impersonate a bomber, to empty the clouds...
Were they superstitious, the engineers who roughed her out?

The day after her official maiden flight Dad wrote our address
on an envelope and licked the stamp. It was months

before she'd break the sound barrier, reach the border
with space and overtake the sunset. I pull my empty letter

from its dusty place; in the address I hear his *Jacqueline*,
the four beats of *3 Stream Farm Close*, the tremor of my teens.

THE FLORIST

Adelaide Street begins in wasteland, ends, for us, at the Florist,
served by the two gay Robins in pinnies and on darts night, thongs,
when teams of men return from Paulsgrove, leaving Portsdown Hill
and its hollowed-out secrets. Olive draws bitter for them –
these shepherds down from summer pasture, home for winter.

Now see us on rooftops or barring the doors of terraced houses,
once lived in by the Paulsgrove men, women and children –
the jaws of bulldozers opening. Demolition crews stand by.

See the two Robins clear a space at a table for a third Robin
(jacket inside-out, eyes flaring with conspiracies and Atlantis)
settling him between men who'd hold him. Olive hushes the pianist.
Where else could we bring him but the Florist? Its lounge,
bottle and jug, snug, public and private bars have heard everything
a family does, everything a boy away from home can imagine.

MY MOTHER'S A GLORIOUS AUTUMN DAY

She outshines last night's frosty moon, settling in her garden
among overgrown shrubs, the lilac tree, digging up tubers

and bulbs to store away, clearing space for a white hydrangea
and a Magnolia stellata whose stars never left their buds.

As I look down at her house, to the east, ribbons of mist
occupy every hollow and dip to the limit of the Downs.

Tonight, in the west the sky will repeat a familiar drama.
What a run of days, so quick, the midday sea silver

for miles, silhouetting the new wind farm's first pegs –
so much silver a freighter could be daubed in it, entering a port

at the end of its passage like a charm, to unload more charms:
women and men in miniature, pallets of shoes, an oak tree,

cow, hands raised in peace, which someone will leave
in a chapel, by a Madonna, as votives, tokens of gratitude.

BANJO AND GLASS JUG

Summer had its own song in the charts –
sing along with us it demanded on the by-pass
towards Winchester, I was 15
and it was my first holiday alone,
my back against a hot car seat
and Ray Dorset, the image of a man I'd meet
years later, his song on the radio dawdling
into my memory, tangling itself up with sun
through glass, one car window open
to rushing hedges, that mid-August smell of tyres on
a sticky road away from home,
yarrow a metre high, smelling of spice –
the summer I missed Hendrix,
and when the rain came, it was torrential.
Minutes when it's all
in place, whatever it is – nothing to do with sex
or happiness, but what's to come. Mystics
know it, the dying too. Last night (ridiculous,
I know) I tried to list the times I might have felt it, curious
to see if I'd summon it. One time comes
close – there was cow parsley over a dried-up stream,
tall, pale, a resting swarm. Someone was cutting
willows behind the house and a chainsaw sputtered.

LOVE SONNET

after Elizabeth Barrett Browning

I came to love and couldn't explain it –
a fox will stare, and those new shoes will rub –
new texts pinging minute after minute
into a string of fairy lights. That pub
on that one night. Love made me a right mess,
babbling homage, darling, babe, amour –
scribbling utter nonsense on my face, yes
and magnified, it led me to your door.
I heard myself repeating I and you,
over again, you and I, to outdo
anyone who was there before. I cut
my hair. Days, and jeans, grew baggier but
love's not why, how, a who or a cipher –
I say love lots, love without reason, more.

I've mended her old linen sheets, inherited her arthritis
and the stopped time of her gold watch.
In my grandfather's open top Sunbeam Talbot she had the look
of Jackie Kennedy in scarf and sunglasses – thin

as boys who guided her to leatherwork in a souk.
By the Seine, she's in black and white. Always single.
And on top of hankies in a bedside drawer,
I found the message from Johnny. He wrote from the boat

one afternoon in 1950. He doesn't mention the sea's glamour,
spray on his skin, the deck which can't ever be cool enough.
He doesn't mention a woman at dinner. Did she imagine
his mouth shaping the characters, a blue envelope

in his hand, the skyline, where there was no land?
She might have opened her box of photos to hear music
they danced to, drowning out the rest of the truth
his letter told. Did she hope by re-reading his words

she'd turn the liner round, replace whites-only beaches
he was heading for, with London's meat queues? How often
did she unfold the paper, trace a pencil's loops and dashes –
his only intimacy on a single page, *be brave*?

Two men, with *native* help, report on each bird they snare.
Starting on the plain, they climb through thorns and cacti,
streams and cloud forest. They list hawks, kites, doves,

note how the stomach of a squirrel cuckoo contains a beetle –
and half way up they catch a single female screech owl. Hear
the flock of swifts they netted in a ruined Spanish cathedral,

a young swallow *far from home*, humming birds feeding
in a blur, a family of nine wrens busy in a hedge. One specimen
left its nest *not more than ten days before.*

I close the book on lost whistles, whirrs, squeaks, trills
and setts, on the dawn chorus unhooked from its skins,
carcasses emptied of sky, skeleton wings spread in cases

that used to be trees, under glass that seizes light like water
but cannot flow. A row of fly-catchers from Angola – five brides
asleep on russet veils. Six green broadbills together on their backs,

their emerald breasts a line of hills, beaks pointing at the sky
like stumps – knotted round each claw is a label and string.
Last, three hatchlings arranged in a nest, forever pleading.

THE BLUE MOON OF MOUAZ AL-BALKHI

Under the Lake of Goodness,
Lake of Luxury,
Lake of Perseverance,

people on railway lines,
motorways, fragile boats,

turning silver

under the Sea of Cold,
Sea of Clouds,
the Foaming Sea.

Let's call tonight's moon

Mouaz

for a young man who walked into the sea –
a buck stepping into a lake to drink –

Mouaz

believing he could swim so far.

LETTER FROM CANTON, CARDIFF 1977

When I became her lodger, Mandy told me there'd be calls
at night, women needing a lift to the refuge and there was a list

of phone numbers pinned to the wall like entry codes
for a clandestine place, tucked away in an undisclosed location,

the way certain research stations never appear on a map.
The address couldn't be written or spoken but sometimes a man

found his woman and children, hammered on the front door
which was reinforced with bolts, the best lock and chains,

while an eye at the spyhole felt the rhythm of his fists.
And I thought of Mandy when I found my friend's letter

from Canton in a folder printed with pavilions and blossom:
He pulled me back by the hair, I fell and he was kicking my head,

I kept thinking of that Dutch guy they're trying for war crimes.
I got to hospital a week after, had a broken finger, several chipped teeth.

My ears were strange for some time. It's been an eventful term.
I don't know what I wrote in reply – nearly 40 years has gone –

but I wish for the young woman she was then, a stone lion,
and for Mandy's broken nights, a walled rose garden.

GRISETTE

She has a face you've seen somewhere, a nurse,
friend of a friend. She'll be whatever you want:
an extra, stand-in, the woman on reception,
a chaperone, guest at the opening making up numbers,
washer-up, cleaner, the dead ringer, the unknown
sightseer in your holiday photo, continuity announcer,
the voice that puts you on hold. Make her up,
like Our Lady of Guadalupe, or the Virgin in Knock.
She'll materialise as bones in a wall, fog from the sea –
your *grisette* of the Belle Epoque with uncertain eyes,
a name that sounds like somebody else.

THE ANCESTORS

are having a summit –
they chase around the garden
disturbing hens.

Silver birches shake,
light shudders
in the branches.

The ancestors try on dresses
delivered by the centuries
they roam through like bandits.

When they speak
it's with the yellow eyes
of a fox and clicks of an orca.

They wrestle, naked,
on the grass
for the best shoes.

Tomorrow they're having a banquet
of possets and pears.
They sit on the table,

whistling *Happy birthday*,
promise to leave white dishes
at your door.

POCKET ST ANTHONY

I am now unable to ease a splinter
from my thumb or read the small print

of terms and conditions. Join a flock of sheep,
people say, or post a prayer to St Anthony

down the back of the sofa. Lost time
and stolen time are gathering behind me

darkening the sky. They will come back
as hail, rain, snow, keeping me inside

to watch the breaking sky and scatter me.

SILVER INKWELL

A thought in the darkness of itself –
could remain complete
in the lake between head and hand.

BOURJOIS

In a box of rouge on a dressing table
and inside the wartime-thin house,
up the dark stairs,
is the sound of a letter
practising how it will end.

MINIATURE TRAY

I used to sit them at a matchbox,
the miniature people
I served from a miniature tray,

held in my voice
so as not to injure their ears
or blow them down.

I opened a hatch into myself,
where I'd look into a cup
and see a horse galloping away.

GEODE

The shepherd builds an image of himself
from stones, tricking sheep, tricking dusk.

He carries what's left of the diamond mine
for sale in his hands. Cars pass

and night bounces back his mineral lights
as lost children and gods.

MALTESE DOLL

Lift the petticoat –
every pleat of her black skirt
is starched with prayer.

Her tiny hands are splayed,
a veil gathers folds
to press down her hair.

Lift the petticoat –
see stitches on her legs,
authentic underwear.

POSTCARD WITH SIX STAMPS

This woman's head staring east
commemorates the invention of gravity.

Sometimes almost all the space for an address

is occupied by a row of heads
lined up for nothing more than a hello.

COPPER BRACELET

The shackle, then, is a survivor.
With the crucifix
it outlasts almost everything.

BROKEN NECKLACE

Even now it deflects red
into the gaps,

like the red blossom in winter
monkeys love to eat,

or rose hips reserving space
for summer in a winter hedge.

BOTTLE OF BILLET DOUX

A sample on the wrist, rubbed on the vein,
will perfume the blood. It's all I want –

my blood replaced
by a love letter from Provence.

LETTER FROM GRAHAM

I drive you in turn to the train – one at 7,
one at 4, come home to stand in your rooms.

I listen for the end of a laugh, text, *Lovely*
to see you twice over, hang up headphones

you've forgotten, shake out your tunes.
Footsteps in the hall belong to my neighbours.

I smell their coffee and toast. When their dog barks
I'm mute as a suitcase, the bath.

The kitchen table's how I leave it – my glasses
look into a polka dot cloth. I'm surprised

how the house doesn't drum, only the cat
composes her scales. I'm grateful for creases in clothes,

hanging like skins to dry off. After work, I hesitate
with Jane, walk home as the sun's consumed by distant estates.

Cyclists remind me of torches flashing through rocks
on the hillside where that tree smells of piss.

There you are at the top, looking down
past me, past your Dad. The silence I open the door on

is felted wool, still as mug, plate and spoon. I creak
into the chill of the loft, and bring down a folder of letters –

Graham has written from Aberdeen *all the love*
in the universe from me and my bicycle chain.

JACKIE WILLS has worked for newspapers, magazines and several universities. A former journalist, she's been a writer in residence in business, schools, arts and community organisations, including Unilever, London Underground, Shoreham Airport, the Surrey Hills, the London Symphony Orchestra and Aldeburgh Poetry Festival. She has been a Royal Literary Fund Fellow and run reading groups.

Over three decades, Wills has organised live poetry events and mentored many emerging writers, consolidating her experience in *The Workshop Handbook for Writers* (Arc, 2016). Her poems feature in several anthologies including *Writing Motherhood* (Seren, 2017) and *Poems of the Decade: An Anthology of the Forward Books of Poetry* (Forward Arts Foundation, 2015). Wills writes short stories and creative non-fiction as well as poetry. She has collaborated over many years with visual artist Jane Fordham and Fabrica Gallery in Brighton.